Dreams of the Dead

DAVID HARSENT

Dreams of the Dead

OXFORD LONDON NEW YORK
OXFORD UNIVERSITY PRESS
1977

Oxford University Press, Walton Street, Oxford OX2 6DP
OXFORD LONDON GLASGOW NEW YORK
TORONTO MELBOURNE WELLINGTON CAPE TOWN
IBADAN NAIROBI DAR ES SALAAM LUSAKA
KUALA LUMPUR SINGAPORE JAKARTA HONG KONG TOKYO
DELHI BOMBAY CALCUTTA MADRAS KARACHI

© David Harsent 1977

British Library Cataloguing in Publication Data

Harsent, David
    Dreams of the dead.
    I. Title
    821'.9'14   PR6058.A6948   77-30082
    ISBN 0-19-211875-7

*Printed in Great Britain by
The Bowering Press Ltd
Plymouth*

To Ian Hamilton

ACKNOWLEDGEMENTS

SOME of these poems have previously appeared in the following publications: *The New Statesman, The New Review, The Times Literary Supplement,* New Poems 1 and New Poems 2 (The Arts Council of Great Britain). *Truce* was first published in a signed, limited edition by The Sycamore Press (Oxford).

CONTENTS

TRUCE

The dust in corners
sheds the scent of almonds.

The window is a mirage
where the dull
planets revolve around their own reflections.

The pattern grows
simpler with study, as she squanders
the last hour before daybreak.

Somewhere, beyond the steel perimeter,
her plane lifts off.

* * *

Memories of the flags,
the flea-market, the music.
Five islands where she lived
a peasant's life for most of one summer.

The icon has a smell I can't detect.
The colours seem to fade as they are watched,
fogged by the tinted lamp, blue becoming grey;
but still the child's nimbus
glows in the pale light.

* * *

Our first drinks
pledge a kind of freedom.
In the lighted windows of courtyard flats,
couples are raising glasses.

Seated on a cushion, glass in hand,
she watches how her Japanese
flower arrangement droops
towards the heat.

Those famished pinks
are all she has to learn by:
love's only accidents.

*   *   *

With dusk, a few stray snowflakes
taking hold
on windowsills and basement steps.

She wipes a bowl with garlic, lights the stove
and lays ingredients
along a glass-topped table.

The main line stations
are full of new arrivals
buttoning coats, and staring at the weather.

Five minutes, maybe less, and they are gone.
Their footprints on the pavement
gather a brittle lace along the rim.

The house grows quiet around her as she works.
The kitchen water
comes straight from the Arctic ice.

*   *   *

The sound of shots.
A burst, silence, a burst.
Cross-legged, dressed to kill
in high boots
and her Guatemalan poncho,
she watches Cybulski
igniting tots of liquor.
Blind souls of the dead
glimmer in the shuttered room.

*   *   *

The lights of the city come on,
blue and orange.
Silhouetting nothing,
they burn like flowers that only bloom at dusk.

Whenever she is ready, they are there,
framed by the window.

The sea; the place of her birth; the lights of ships.

*   *   *

Perhaps it was
an act of courage simply being there,
knee-deep in the blinding white.

The photograph
shows her flanked by trees filled to the brim
with snow, like goblets;

3

she is gazing
away to the left, composed against
a perfect backdrop.

Her cigarette,
dabbed against the fire's filament,
browns along its length.

'That winter
was the last of things,' she says
and frowns, and feels ashamed.

*   *   *

The two sisters across the street
spend all day in the kitchen.
Their dark, identical shawls
smudge the window as they watch the stove.

Below their balcony
an awning flaps like a sail.
A man in dove-grey linen gloves
is sweeping sodden leaves over the kerb.

Sunday afternoon.
Her future falls into place.
She smiles at the thought, then comes awake
for the aftertaste of limes along her tongue.

*   *   *

4

Denim and pearls; her nails
left untouched;
her eyes in the ancient style.

The one blank wall
is freckled with morning sunlight:
maps of last night's promises,

a circus in Isfahan, a pine forest,
the drive cross-country
to avoid the rains.

Her palm-print
shrinks on the mirror as she turns away.
The day is spoken for.

* * *

Closed shutters; doorsteps growing grass;
the twilit stillness of deserted hallways.

Attics strewn with the broken ghosts of sheeting,
with family albums, relics of a war,

and toys preserved intact by gifted children:
the quiet, abandoned things of settled lives.

Rooms she imagines. Worlds beyond her own.

Disturbed by silences, she lies awake
trying to recall what fixed her here.

5

A lullaby, perhaps, the smell of uncut lupins,
a bus ride, a refusal, lines of spray
along a sea-wall, milk in brown stone jugs.

*   *   *

She comes in past the heavy gilded mirror
smiling, wearing a wide blue hat.
I rise and start to speak. The door closes.

She enters the room again, smiling,
wearing a foxfur and the wide blue hat.
When I speak
my words fade on the air; the door glides shut.

She comes into the room,
smiling, wearing the hat, the foxfur,
and I rise.
                —My dream about the room.

Now she comes in, slowly, balancing
honey in a dish and melon slices.

*   *   *

Dog-tired, but somehow keeping track,
she sets up small objections to the music
but lets it play.

Crouched by the fire
she soon ceases to listen;
her eyes are watching something miles away.

If nothing's changed
an hour from now, we've won:
survivors of the wind, the streaming glass,
the life outside.

Endurance

The orchard is lit
on one side by the evening sun.
Its yellows glow.
An odour of leaves and rind pours in.

Hillsides are dealing with last year's scars—
endurance of the just-visible.
Twin children, hair ablaze,
number the lunatic eyes of moon daisies.

It is the true magic.
In the pause between mind and movement
history claims its own.

Dog Days

Summer's high-spots are burned out.
The dry slopes facing south
bear trenches of black, scorched into the stubble.

The boy watches his nurse
as she confiscates the flowers. Her hands are stained
just above the wrist. She smiles her smile.

The sheets warm, sun on the windows opposite
blurring at the corners of his eyes,
he feels his senses losing ground.

The house filling with murmurs.
A drift of woodsmoke past the glass.
The *chink* of bottles brought from the cellar's coolness.

Children's Hour

The girl and the flowers are pale inseparables.
Abandoned to the blues and dusty yellows,
half-sister to the white
shadow in the window-pane,
she watches the sleek Arapahoes
fight back across a dozen Godless acres.

Luggage

Your Gothic Christ is fake, but beautiful,
the rigid nose,
the perfect mouth for kissing.

You kept it always, travelling light
for seven years
until ambition finally slowed you down.

The Cornish badlands soaked up three-day storms
and never softened—
you couldn't believe your luck.

Day after day
you struggled in to paint.
That sad girl made us tea: delicately red; the pungency
of lemons.

Fishbowl

For Fred Taylor

1

A couple are stepping out on platform four;
his campaign ribbons gleam, her breasts
roll beneath the satin. Nests
of tourists spread their maps out on the floor.
The patterns alter. There's a law
that governs departures, and one that governs murders.
In the gloom of the roof workmen are welding girders.

2

A 'northern airstream' puckers the parkside trees.
The animals in the zoo lean on their bars
or pace in heady circles. No-one sees.
The rich arrive, downy in perfect furs,
at theatres with neon-etched marquees.
The wind that killed the Brontës. Iron spears
ring the wolf enclosure. There are pleas
for one more encore from the velvet tiers.

3

The bald man mutters across the rim of his glass
to the girl in the stetson; she has brought her dog.
They're nothing special. Except for the sunny gloss
on his skull, they'd be lost in the multicoloured clog
of drinkers and talkers. The neatly bevelled fosse,
that drains into the river, froths with ale
and scraps of muddied bunting from the farce
(the players have left, taking their cash-on-the-nail).
The party revolves like a slowly sinking wreck.
'Perfection . . .' he whispers, resting a hand on her neck.

4

Couple by couple, they find their place in the dark.
The girls know how to glide beneath a touch:
sleek and unevolving, like the shark.
The piano-player downstairs knows too much
about the gritty business of the skin;
even so, he likes to leave his mark.
Angling her knees, she reaches to guide him in.
He yelps as his spreading fingers brush her fin.

5

Sheep nudge and nibble the pallid downs. The hare
circles, in a frenzy, back to where
women in bowlers and breeches are crossing a stream,
flexing their thighs as they hear the quarry scream.
The bank is pocked with the marks of paws and studs
that will garner scabs of ice from the freezing air.
The season is right for worshipping cruel gods.
On a mattress of coats, acting a part from a dream,
Wednesday's child is screwing his girl in the woods.

6

She smiles and smiles at his raw, grogblossomed face.
Smiling makes the good times come.
Dance-floor partners stall and change the pace,
their stomachs touching and their heads in space.
His dampened finger tamps a crumb:
he licks it, gives his empty plate a shove,
and looks up smiling. All we know of love
is pain and the response to pain.
They waltz in the old-fashioned way, with impulsive grace;
he leans back to speak, and she smiles again.

7

Laughter in the Wendy house, a ghost
of someone's face reflected in the pane.
Love provides the terrors that we hide,
then seek . . . the party's nerveless host.
The scents that gather in the gathering rain
bleed off from the garden like a tide,
spilling across the pavement. Parents ride
in convoy to the house; insane
visions make them shudder as they coast
along the driveway: lights through a seepage of fog.
The children hoard their secrets, safe and smug.

8

They are slender-waisted, blonde, with eyes like glass.
Lodged in the grass, they watch for rival styles.
She smiles as he gets up on his knees to piss.
Crook a finger at bliss and music storms
between the tents where, adorned in pretty rags,
she sighs and sags against his bony chest,
rumpling a nest amid their tangled rugs.
Sometimes he begs; she sometimes flirts with theft.
His pinkie browses the cleft between her legs.

DREAMS OF THE DEAD

April 30

The women started downhill from the crest
sidling against the slope, their skirts
lifted at the hip,
their braided hair
releasing wisps of light into the wind.

The morning opened out with blues and golds,
the smell of chlorophyll.
                        The sun
strung opal beads along
his eyelash as he woke.

*   *   *

May 2

Hottest near the surface: vast white arcs in space
the sunspots crack in blackness.
Tidy in bed, his arms and legs aligned,
he recalled how swifts will sleep while on the wing:
a night-long, dreamless glide.

The room grew warmer. Dust rose in the sunlight.
Opposing mirrors, blank
and fathomless as water,
waited for his image while he slept.

*   *   *

May 7

Jungfrau. Snow slopes near the peak.
Each snapshot slightly fogged
by cloud and background movement.
Inside the Ice Palace
light struck in frosty lines across his eyes,
the silence like a hood.

Thousands of feet below
thin streams lace the lower slopes.
Sure-footed on the scree, the women move
down towards the foothills, the altitude of songbirds.

*　　*　　*

May 9

Like spiders' webs unpicking,
something crackled deep inside his lungs.
Those mornings when his hands shook
and that same
bitterness rose in his mouth,
he let the dreams fade as he roamed the house.
The slow roll of a cypress in his garden,
or a crease
of rain across the glass, would be enough
to turn his thoughts.
　　　　　　Then coffee and the papers:
the fire in Asia, the small world of statistics.

*　　*　　*

May 15

Mornings arrived with tiny gaps in meaning.
The spring winds dropped at dawn:
time for the garden's old inhabitants
drifting between
the glistening boles of pear trees.
Remnants of the first rain jostled down
from branch to leaf, splitting the early sunlight.

'I live for those moments when we both
forget ourselves.'
                    He dreamed he woke,
seeing first the waxy curlicue
of a lily under glass,
a pomander,
a painted eggshell resting by the mirror.

For a moment he held them in focus.
Old bargains. The death wish in women.
When, finally, he surfaced from the dream
the streets were dry, the morning almost done with.

*   *   *

May 21

Albino. Poor child. He tiptoes through playtime,
his bloodless head
in negative against the wood's penumbra.

Where the sun strikes back
from the blazing cruciform of the chalk excavations,
he almost disappears.

His constant companion, that dark boy,
crosses the wiry turf
at a dead run, his brown hair smudged with leaf-dust.

The women smile, shielding their eyes to watch.
They are laying out
fruit and wine and bread on a damask cloth.

* * *

May 22
One mirror is sealed over by the sun,
a brittle barrier
where something is trembling for release.

A flight of doves, lit on their undersides,
wheel into view, then clatter overhead.
Too tired for that, he lets his eyes slide shut.
Fragments of retina
swim up beneath the lids.

* * *

May 31

Five massive rocks
chopped the undertow to ragged
bursts against the blue;
that vicious seething was the only sound.

On the farthest lip of sand,
a flutter of colour, the women's parasols
spread pools of shade. Softer than breath,
a pulse ticked in his temple as he watched

then turned and went full-tilt
towards the breakers. Engulfment in that green
drifting light took hours: the throb of water,
the mild tug of the tide rolling him on.

*　　*　　*

June 2

His senses trapped,
he watched the views float back,
sharp-edged and colour-perfect.

Most of one night, sleeping and awake,
rehearsing someone else's tragedy.
The late train to the coast,
the mourners grouped
on one side of the treeless, cliff-top graveyard;
and then, at dusk, the house awash with light,
a figure on the terrace
standing still, listening for the rhythm of the sea.

That sound set him afloat, his body caught
the motion of the swell.
A figure on the terrace,
looking out.
The salt taste of the child's lips.

*　　*　　*

June 7

Above the slender elms, the local-stone
period chimneystacks,
the spire cut a wedge into the sky.

Lightning always struck there first.

A man had died one night,
drunk and desperate,
roped to its perfect profile. The churchyard crows
scored his cheeks next day
before the thatching ladders could be brought.

A peal of six bells, echoes into echoes.

Was that a dream as well?—
The Virgin's mantle in the eastern window
staining the steepled hands;
the women's veils
stirring as they mouthed the first responses.

*   *   *

June 9

Early-morning cloud banks nudged the hills,
the underside of heaven,
misting the true vanishing point,
the point of departure.
                     The blues and blacks in nature
absorbed him: those shadows, the stiffening wind,
and then the first thin stalks of light.

Rays to redden women's hair, a breeze to make it fly!
Unimaginable, the solar winds
roared through space, putting the earth awry.

*   *   *

June 10

For seconds at a time, his mind stopped dead.
Not faints, not *petit mal*; a loss of will
perhaps. He shuddered, then emerged.

Three nights without sleep had left him dull.
It seemed his friends, his generation, dwindled; some
had made a case for love—

the age would not permit it.
                                        'But it's you
I fear for most. What's to become
of your life now?'
                            A memory of the sea,

the southern rip-tides,
filled his head with noise.
His night-light dipped and flared behind the glass.

                    *   *   *

June 12

Eyes bright with fatigue, he walked to where
trees scattered the glare, a roil of leaves
flowing along the bough.

Six horses cropped the downland.
A gleam like silk
travelled their flanks. He dozed and watched.

In single file
the women left the treeline,
a flicker at the corner of his eye.

He blinked. They passed between
a stone wall and the wheatfields
into the shade, the blue bowl of the valley.

*   *   *

June 20

The children's voices teased him,
always just beyond
the next dune, or the next warp of the cliff.
How long ago was that? They learned
to walk lopsided on the pebbles
towards the shimmer where the sea fell back,
a mist of blue and amber.

He dreamed the place again:
in moonlight, calm, deserted, with a sea
flat, black and frangible.
And all at once
was certain of a desperate energy
beneath that placid surface—
of a form,
teeth clenched against the salt,
swimming upwards, wildly, through the dark.

*   *   *

June 23

The summer lasted, month to month.
Neighbourhood children tanned
and ran the streets till evening.
His household glass
beamed chips of rainbow on the walls and ceilings.

All brightness taxed him;
the blinding linen
that lapped his face each morning,
the glance that scorched his eye,
the inexhaustible
crystal at the centre of the sun.

*   *   *

June 25

He broke
eggs into a pan and watched them settle,
perfectly smooth, a fleck
of brighter red in one; energy arrested.

(The sounds of five a.m.:
birdsong out of blackness,
a wind riffling the orchard).

The dreams that spoiled his sleep
still kept their hold:
the kitchen—warm with cooking—
hung everywhere with women's implements.

*   *   *

24

July 3

The sweep of their skirts leaves tracks in the morning wet.

One whistling a tune, and one
hanging back from the rest
to watch a poppy's petals smudge to mauve
as they are torn . . .

Brightness like a backwash draws them on.

Bones into chalk. Pelts into melting pap.
Victims of the twilight kills
treading to mulch and fragments underfoot . . .

They harbour a gift: decades of memories.

Their high-necked blouses dampen,
a pool
of moisture at the hollow of the throat;
the cling of cotton at their calves and thighs.

What ripens is their flesh . . .

The wakening town hangs in a pale haze
beyond the valley's rim;
they keep it always in sight.
A pair of swifts are shuttling across the blue.

*   *   *

July 9

An ensign in his dreams,
the storm beacon
flew each day above the tallest outcrop.
Each day
the sky's first flush turned indigo by noon
and a wind poured in from the sea.
                              The house
stood four-square to the weather, windows flexed,
the verandah's raddled stanchions
soaking up stain.
                   That much was familiar:
light teeming across the bay,
a building rooted in stone,
a figure on the terrace, looking out.

Later, the focus altered—something new—
to sandflats furrowed by the ebb,
gulls and clouds and shallows,
inshore rocks,
all fixed, an instant, in the frame.
And barely visible in so much space,
that form, beached on the dunes,
shrouded by seagrass,
pungent with shells and brine.

*   *   *

July 15

He lay in the sun, motionless through the day,
a blizzard of red
roaring behind his eyes, while his skin
tightened and dried.

—The scorch that withers greenness, melts
the flesh from cattle, leaving them bones and leather,
that burns its starvelings,
bleached the orchard at its boundaries.

That night he shed a glow,
a child with a fever needing a woman's touch.
The solar gold
flooded his sleep, the whole life of the dream.

*　　*　　*

July 20

His sleeping eye
flickered to show the white; he saw
his own feet tamping grass, and pale moths
rising from the stalks.

He traced the lip of the hill by its darker line
on the sky's near black.
Miles beyond that ridge
the streets of the village were strung with coloured lamps

raising a glow, like beacons starting up
on peaks above the farmland.

The chalk slopes on the sheer side of the hill
were struck with the shadows of trees.

He waited for the sense of place to come
as the first flare cracked and rose

*   *   *

July 20

a sudden livid red
dipping towards the shore.

The cliff-edge slick with spray, the signal fires
flattened to orange circles by the wind,
acres of cumulus
streaming off the skyline . . .

Just to stand full-face watching the sea
numbed him with effort.
He knew the rest, a drama of repetitions:
death by drowning,

the drift and muffle of narcosis.
The body washed in,
a froth of limbs and spume across the rocks.
He screamed and seemed to wake.

*   *   *

July 23

Insects
ticked against the glass
or found the open fanlight,
trailing in
a flicker of tendril legs.
From somewhere in the house, the sound
of water trickling.

'If you die, I'll hear of it
and arrive to parade the churchyard
in my blue hat
pinned with flowers.'

The day assembled clear shapes in the heat,
outlines and edges;
colours sharpened through the early haze.

'What more
can love do to us now?'

*   *   *

July 24

The day gone grey with rain,
a thinner spray
blown like spindrift through the fall;
each room uninhabitable
as if the house had seen a death.

29

A keen eye could have picked them out
in moments when the downpour slackened,
crossing a high field beyond the town,
ranged like climbers.

He meandered back to bed,
wanting to sleep.
The whole eastern valley wall
glowed as beaded water caught the light—
luminous green when the cloud broke.

*   *   *

July 29

Tiny scavengers broke cover
from sour corners of the kitchen garden.

His room built heat
behind sealed windows; roof beams cracked and settled.

There were piles of books
stacked beside the bed. There were ashtrays,

soiled clothes, the sightless mirrors.
There was his small collection of knives.

'. . . you are talking of freedoms I haven't come to yet.
Nothing abides. But the days out here seem endless . . .'

*   *   *

August 6

They smile at the prodigal: women of the house.
Love and the warm brick and gulls on the lumpy fields;
nature feeding and the autumn dregs.

It dimmed and went awash,
as if his eye
had filled with blood or caught the flooding sunset
running red on hanging copper pans.

*   *   *

August 13

Blind and numb, wrapped in the caul of blankets.

He woke in fear,
seeing at once the widening pool of sky
smudged with small birds that twitched in ragged flocks
from pane to pane.
                 The evening before
his eye had followed the tracks in the half-grown crops
that seemed to flow back to a second, deep horizon.

Was that dreaming?
The daze of concentration, his slowing pulse,
the spire's knife-edge against the thinning blue . . .

*   *   *

August 23

The orchard beyond his window took the sun,
blurring the edge of everything.
It stunned him to look. The wash of distances.

In the spaces between the trees at the outer edge
the women waited, the light
lancing the colour from their eyes.

How strange, to love only the dead.
There was nothing to hear or touch;
there was nothing to be kept—

the room and its brutal ornaments,
his jumbled books,
the mirrors dissolving in each other's gaze.

He stepped into the vast, unshuttered glare
like a swimmer loosing his foothold,
moving through silence, his own element.

Bodinnick

'Love God and work the sea.'
His raven's voice
rasped from the pulpit.
Shadows spread in the chancel.

In the granite caverns
off Lantivet Bay
drowned men jostled stalactites;
their eyes, scoured by salt,

looked inland, where you set
your face against a gale
along the cliff-walk,
richness underfoot: wren's bones,

lardings of kelp,
the dusty, mouldering hides.
From the harbour, we watched you
dwindle on planes of blue.

Fishermen, like penitents,
trudged the shoreline
waiting on a tide,
the great shoals massing,

a sudden heave
of silver against the swell.
At twilight, diesel smoke
rose on the hill like ground-fog.

The child laughed in his sleep.
Hooded, you withdrew
into a flush of rain,
the cobbled squares around the quay,

palming a cigarette,
then returned with that dead look.
We lay above
the dull lights of the village

silent, burning with loss,
hearing the house beams creak,
the long tremor of rollers
ringing the corner stones.

Birds Hunting the Outskirts

The city is cooling; the hills outside the city cool,
where the bright-eyed hunters wheel
to quarter the open slopes.

The silhouettes at single windows are
the city's midnight, bruised insomniacs,
alive to the growing silence
and opening to the sodium glare like flowers.

Night-fear tunes their nerves:
something like hunger, something like love,
music in the cortex,
the heroic moment when the bone breaks.

Foxface, the final hour, the hiss of wings.
In their brilliant steel apartments,
their lissom cars,
they won't leave death alone.

Birds Roosting in Bad Weather

By midday there was something in the sky
like the smudge of another galaxy.
Everything cooled and darkened,
umbra along the tunnels of the maze, shadows greening a pool,
the garden's Dionysus, dulled.

The very edge of the rainstorm brushed the trees,
feather and leaf;
and if someone had stood in the lee of the sandstone wall,
smoking, perhaps,
and sweetening her teeth with an apple,
that fateful letter crushed in her raincoat pocket,
she might have watched the first spread of the lightning
over the backdrop grey
and birds riding the blackened twigs in silence,
fire and flesh that nobody can own.

Birds Flocking on Lindisfarne

That reckless voice, high-pitched, right through the night
and wind belling the darkness . . .
He chipped away at something in his workroom.

Next day, driving north,
he almost killed them both on one tight bend
(she moaned as the wicked drift hollowed her spine)
then they were on the causeway:
seabed boulders,
weed swaying like crops on either side.

As if a year had passed
they modelled themselves against the granite skyline,
haunch by haunch,
she with her queenly smile
letting him put his hand inside her dress.

The first gull came
racing out of the sun in a pure curve;
and then the rest—
shrill, fine-boned hysterics—mobbed the shore,
enraged by the scent of leavings in the surf.

Level 7

The lamps of the terminal cases burn till dawn.

* * *

The last of the storm
trails into the morning's undertow.
'Up here there are no horizons; we sleep among clouds
or watch the night sky, like renegades, for a signal.'

* * *

Ancient walls hold up under the weather, their granite roots
locked into the hillcrest; the city fathers are there
under chiselled slabs, serenely falling to pieces.
A century's corruption darkens the stonework.
Each evening, visitors' cars whine up that hill
kindling the crumpled windows, irrigating patterns of frost on
                                                    iron.
Convalescents watch them hit the rise, headlight beams
toppling into the valley—then the whole sad convoy
cruising the outskirts . . . love in the guise of fear,
hands closing on one another, cut flowers staining their tissue.

* * *

'. . . it was long ago, too long to get things straight;
in another part of the country . . . and the people are gone.
So frail—I think my flesh could crumble,
flaking away from the bone like something cooked . . .

38

I only remember
the moments of deceit . . . that sudden shout of laughter
from the lawn outside my window; and later the girl
coming into my room, white as a fish,
smoking with powder after her morning bath . . .'

*   *   *

The cloudless, endless blue begins to tear.
Instruments scald in their vats. The first drugs of the day are
                              soaking through.
Stars make soft explosions beyond the dampened glass, their
                              glimmer shrinks
back into space, a final rush of light
where the rim of the universe thrums like a wire in the wind.

*   *   *

Birds are thronging the undergrowth. Pale rods of sunlight
root among the groundsman's hothouse tulips.
In a shuttered room, an Italian orderly sings
as he washes the limbs of the new dead. Healers
with brain-cells in their fingertips
greet the day with knives . . . floodlights swamping the tile,
the blemished faces ebbing under gas.

At the Solstice

The lip of ice
yaws, enticing black runnels,
then the pane
splits with a sweet crack.

Frozen in. Your sinew
melted; but I imagine you
staring straight up
out of the cloak of hair

and subsoil litter,
fingers laced on your breast,
the impossibly long,
perfectly fluted nails.

We buried you
in the blizzard of '63.
It's an accident, coming back
in this feathery rush of snow,

the year's first ice-wind
strengthening with the dusk.
I needed a map
to find you. My youngest child

stamps tiny cleated footprints
along your neat verge
and examines the bright
curl of his breath on the air.

I've been afraid for so long,
laid-up in that place . . .
Nothing could cool me,
the sisters of steel

plied at my bedside,
gleaming and pleased to be there.
Each time I woke
with their voices hard at my head,

their talents were sprouting inside me.
As the needle drove in
and I counted backwards from ten
they would smile at each other, keepers

of some forgotten art.
The wickerwork cornucopia
spilled on my locker,
arranged as for Caravaggio;

the death tents
were pitched along the ward,
steamy with sickness. In each,
a crumpled pink bud, bedded down.

Drugged and reassured,
I can think of nothing to ask for.
These scattered flowers
are already brown and crusty,

little enough to add
to your deep dream of riches.
Light-footed on the frosty stone,
the Godly glide past

to Evensong: the few
friends who outlived you.
The pure note of the choir
calls them in,

the tapers, the purple and gold,
the gloss of decadence.
Like you, like them, I shall grow
each day more distant,

watching the future close down,
sensing malevolence
in weather, in rough dreams,
the old portents.

My voice will crack
the clear syllables;
my children will watch me, and let me
pretend to earn their love.

Mr Punch

The tiercel feathers upwind
breasting the airstream;
there's game on the slopes.

Guests on the valley floor
spread their picnic cloths—
midgets warped by the midday haze.

In the tangle of brush near the pines
unseen animals go belly-down,
hot beneath their tawny pelts.

White linen on the furze,
ribbons and flags,
sky-line clouds a belladonna blue.—

The stasis breaks. A child
is tapping a wineglass on his teeth.
His friends join hands to dance

as lust explodes in the bracken.
Mr Punch worms into the girl
and she squeals like a peccary.

Over his shoulder she glimpses
the hunting bird
and mottled depths of sky

while her blood heats.
Mr Punch is growling; the breeze
cools the sweat on his flanks.

His wife and family feast
and watch the dancers.
These women are all alike to Mr Punch.

He'd like to own them, he'd like to eat them whole,
he'd like their murders
feeding his night-time conscience.

This one's something special:
she loves a dare
and Punchinello thrives on secrecy.

Suddenly, horses are there on the hillside,
standing on their shadows to feed;
distant, they seem to be

behind a wall of glass;
they peel off, circling the dark patches of clover.
A dozen faces look up

struck through with happiness.
White light flashes from silverware,
the wineglass sings

along its breaking-line.
Mr Punch emerges, grinning.
The children dance in their ring.

Punch and the Judy

He feels so old, something primordial,
something that surfaced through the permafrost
sliding blindly towards warmth . . .
icy against her back: she dreams herself
diving through breakers in a winter sea.

Rain at three and rain again at seven,
hanging leaden in the tidy square.
Dawn after dawn—detritus from the whirlpool,
the spars and splinters of shipwreck.
Walls of water roar beside the windows.

The girl's blonde head is drawn
into a caul of weed
and her long legs trawl the dark.
His shoulders rap the bedrock. There comes
a noise like singing as their bodies sunder.

Picked over by dabbing fish.—
Her plump lips on his face and on his neck,
dampness of hair uncoiling.
His mind comes loose: he sees a figure
out on the drowning streets,

camouflaged by morning twilight,
watching the room, his eyes
luminous, like an assassin's.
Her shadow runs on the curtain, then she floats—
a tangle of pink and gold on frosted glass.

Love is his energy and his trap, spurring
the thug beneath the skin: homunculus
hooknosed, hunchbacked . . . Her voice
rings in the shower . . . It stirs in its cage of ribs,
inarticulate and murderous and mad.

Mr Punch Looks Good in Black

Quicklime in the pit, that's more his style.
But comes to lay his wreath with all the rest.
Lilies, of course;
the flower of voided passion.

His lumpy shadow flickers on and off
between avenues of stone angels.
Their mossy hair, their weathered vestments, fly
in the fierce, dry wind. Their eyes
stare into the sun.

Long after the largo has ended, he feels
the notes in his skull.
They chime along his spine.
These are the burnt days of July, the world
gathered under glass, a smell of tinder.
Columns of birds rise from the silt of rivers.
Each hot midday
he downs a bottle and prays for a quiet mind.

Is Punch a killer? Nights alone in the house
leave him shaken and sick.
Prowlers pad the blistered alleyways;
lean and angry, their nerves strung tight,
they own the streets and carve out what they want.
He seems to hear
her voice, a murmur, almost out of earshot
in one of the rooms where her things still lie about.

Less and less the days come back to him—
diminishing, musical. Less and less
the combers of the nearby, blank Atlantic
hold powers to sooth or snare him in their rhythms.
Our sins, our monument. He stumbles through clumps
of eelgrass: sand and the tumbled refuse of the sea,
threads of carbon
racing in his veins. *Suppose*
we could find our place with the living.
Whisky-blind, he thinks the sea is ice:
so flat, blue-green, and burning, like the sky.
Churchbells sound in the depths;
the shockwave of their round
booms above his head and swells
over his cry and the endless din of gulls.

MOMENTS IN THE LIFETIME
OF MILADY

I

The island grasses were filled with unknowable scents
and the flurry of creatures running before her footfalls.
Even at dusk, the nub of the crumbling abbey
was a view on the eastern side.

On knees and palms, swaybacked like a stricken runner,
her skirt thrown up to billow across her back,
she begged, 'Pleasure me, pleasure me.'

He half-understood what she meant. As he worked
he looked out over the broad back of the island,
its lumps of ruin, its rockfalls to the sea.

2

They are gone, she thought, *my pale cavaliers are gone.*
Dogfights in the blue, the silken scarves,
the music after midnight.

How I miss them. Ice in the vein. A goblet's bowl
sang beneath her finger
as the room grew truly sensitive to sound.

She invoked a silence with cool dribbles of wine.
In its niche, her portrait drank light,
ambers and black, and green in the drape of her shawl.

3

Wading through clear water, her body foreshortened
to tits and tuft and her feet spread on the chalk.

The convoys had slowed them, rolling up to the border
under a veil of dust. The last of Europe's summer;
the scum of the earth dividing the earth between them.

The sleeper on the bank sweated his wine.
My paramour. His city had grown dull,
his voice, each morning, a clutter of vowels . . . 'Tesoro . . .'
She arched in a dive and swam for the riverbed,
a pale shape, sounding, sleek enough to be fished.

4 *Berlin, 1949*

Lovers hung like shades in the bar-room glass,
faceless in one another's grip.
She raised her drink to give them 'happy days'.
Offstage, the Joker winked a violet eye
and stripped amid the bottles and the smoke.

A sky of purple flock, the lights, the towers . . .
Later that night, on the Bridge of Unity,
she watched the city die down;
unstrung by the brittle stares of the enemy,
the unopened letters in her hotel bedroom.

5

The barrels moved left to right, a perfect track,
and then the birds went ragged in the air,
bombing the black stubble.— Ultramarine,
September's washy sun on her back;
she moved amid the crossfire like a cat,

pulse jamming her wrist, a purple arc,
tributary to the flood
that funnelled through her womb. Gunshots
banged in her brow,
hosannas racked the trees. *The old*
drool onto their pillows; this fierceness is lost them.

6 *After Giacometti*

The deceived—they are the true obsessives.
That night, her smile
had finally wilted beneath the driveway lanterns.

She was always going to remember
the way the old couple and the children stood
between the whitewashed pillars

and how, as she moved, they dwindled to wire and wax
in the bolts of light
where their heads and hands were fixed.

It was spring, she noticed; the damp had a smell of the sea.
The gardener's sapling birches caught the night wind,
swooping shadows on black.

7

Her yellow roadster stood in the drumming rain,
a mist of white along its canvas top.
Inside the spinney a cool damp conjured smells,
blood-world of the weasel and the shrike
where she bunched her skirt and spread her knees in a squat.

The old life made her feverish:
a drone of voices from the lawn, rich wines,
father's chessboard set for play in the summerhouse;
the family bound to its ritual of sorrow.

Now she was clean away.
The day ebbed in her spine as she watched the stream
trickle between her feet into the thorns.
Smoke among the roots; meat on the spike.
A bludgeon came at the trees . . . She could still taste
sugar from the child's kiss.

8

Rustling in the sill, the spider's ghost dance.
The place was for those who trust severity,
a whisper of salt on stone.

She brooded on her demesne,
mistress of the house, its oaks and velvets,
the garden's stems and saturated apples.

Her deathbed silks
slid from their tissue to drift across her palm.
What sin to hoard them! What peace to be beguiled!

9 Madrid, Joselito

Thinning pearl above an even skyline
where the storm was pulling back;
her train clattered towards it
through acres of orange groves and bamboo windbreaks.

That afternoon, half-choked by the heat,
she'd watched the gipsy killer take his bull,
gliding across the horns.

Christ, how I hate the south. Warm rain like floss,
the baking, purple dusks,
the women in their blacks, courting betrayal.
The train flushed dogs from the scrub. *I'll change my life.*

10 *K622*

Static drowned out the first few bars—
a feint; and then that clarity like sunlight.

The arm that looped her neck
flexed and relaxed. Watching as he dozed

she felt the music clutch . . .
Nothing would save them from the plans they made

at that first rendezvous.
Their deep, slow-burn to frenzy made her ill.

11

She licked the fontanelle . . . the boneless limbs
stirred and lifted like underwater stalks;
a thread of blue
tapped and tapped to irrigate an eyelid.

53

It was thus in dreams, it was thus
in all her best imaginings: the child
taking his strength in sleep,
his dampness on the muslin, the scent of milk.

Beyond the starched reflections in the window
the compound's orange glare
lapped the high fences. Madness on her lip.

12

They kept the room slammed shut against the heat.
Day-long twilight, her body a pale smudge,
spreadeagled, as he brought the cigarettes, the wine.

She watched him pour, then pause; some bleakness struck him;
he stared as if his face had emptied out.
Too late: the sudden, chill suspicion

of bad luck in the blood.
As he moved on her again, she softly spat
three times into his mouth, and sealed her passion.

13

Worn, worn to an edge, her eyes burned out,
salt in the reddened creases of her skin,
beyond words for it all, beyond weak dreams of peace
or deliverance, she drove at a tipsy crawl
to the house in Oxford, clipping kerbs,
dazed by the sunset puddling in the road.

All the old things—she toured the place like a stranger:
amazed; it was cold and intact;
her garden nudging the doorways,
dark ooze by the apple tree stippled with massive paw-prints.

'Wolves,' he laughed, 'wolves,' as they stretched on her
childhood bed.
Later, he posed her by an open window,
preparing the light, icy colours of disdain.
'Keep that whole side tense. Keep looking down.'
—Into the garden, half-hoping to see
a ruff of hackles sloping past the gateway.

14

A three-day downpour, dissolving hills in mist.
After the abandoned conversations,
the sound of water like a long echo.

Sometimes, late at night,
she could almost abandon every wanton scheme . . .
dozy with drink, as the cats
arched and circled before the open fire.

'We are exiled here,' the young man heard her say.